This Book Is Dedicated
To My Parents
Who Always Knew
It Was Possible

Imagine dawn at Sea

A school of fish makes a sudden turn
like a thousand shiny dimes spun from heads to tails.

Imagine sunrise at sea.

A pair of seahorse hover over the ocean floor
like slow dancing puppets with invisible strings.

Imagine daybreak at sea.

A stingray flies through the ocean currents
like a new kite riding through a spring breeze.

Imagine morning at sea.

A flying fish swims through the air in an arc
like a rainbow soaring through a midsummer sky.

Imagine high noon at sea.

A seal speeds toward the sea's surface
like a white rocket rushing to the milky way.

Imagine afternoon at sea.

A sea urchin rests on a coral reef
like a porcupine napping on a bed of spring flowers.

Imagine evening at sea.

A horseshoe crab swishes her tail back and forth like a windshield wiper on a dashboard of sand.

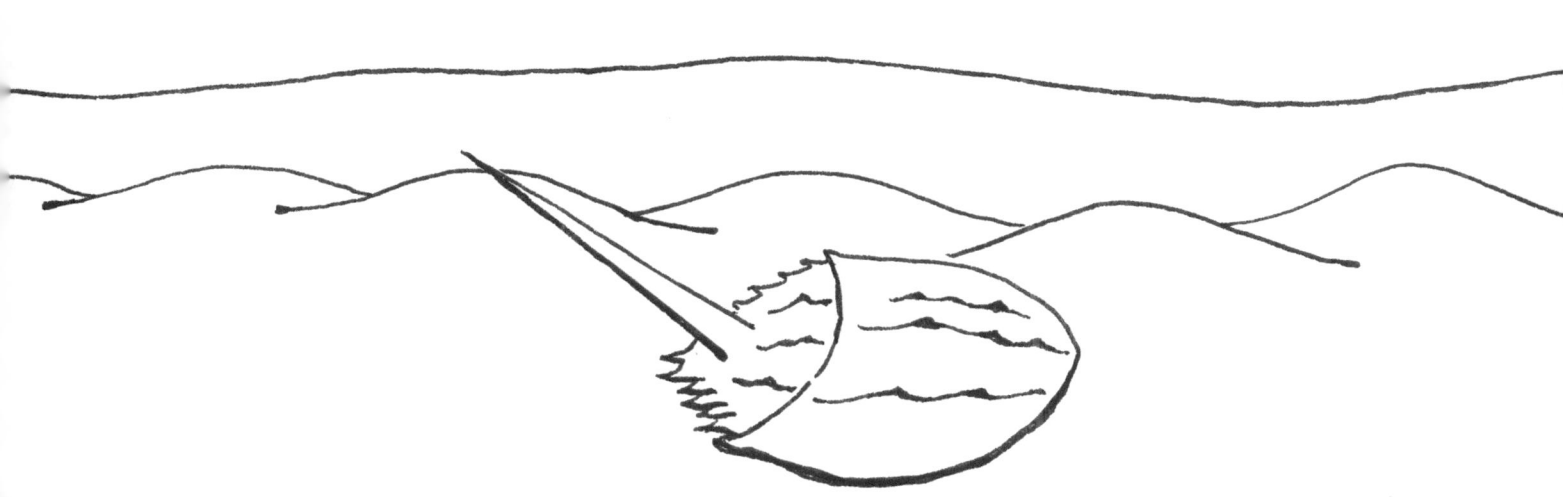

Imagine sunset at sea.

A duo of narwhals tap tusks
like a pair of knights preparing to duel.

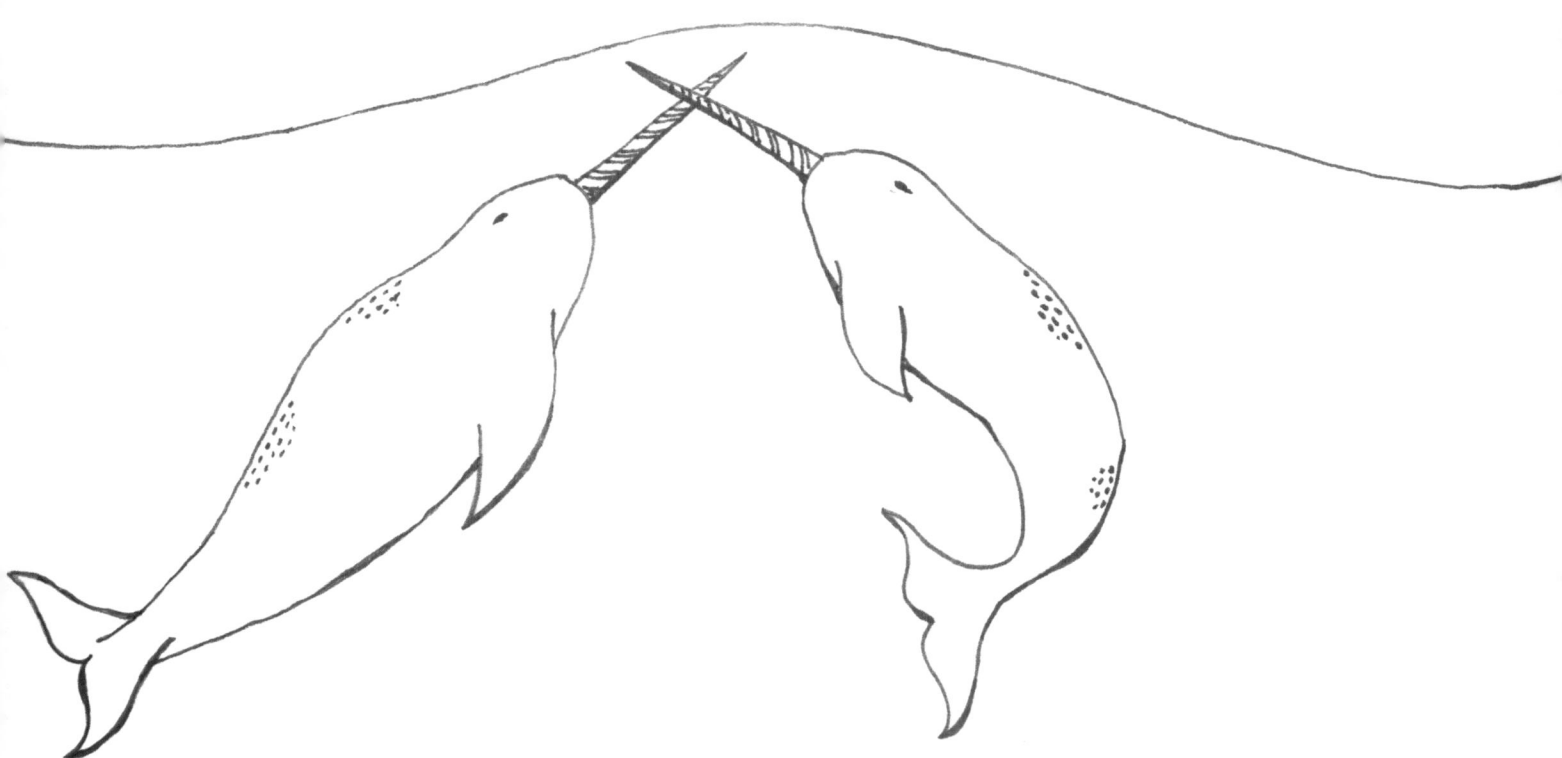

Imagine twilight at sea.

An octopus floats through tranquil waters
like a giant smoke puff rising from a chimney.

Imagine moonrise at sea.

Jellyfish ignite the dark vasty deep
like a field full of fireflies flashing at dusk.

Imagine midnight at sea.

A swordfish slices through inky blue water
like a shooting star racing through a cloudless night sky.

Imagine moonset at sea.

A baby whale swims beside her mother
like the moon itself, following the earth.

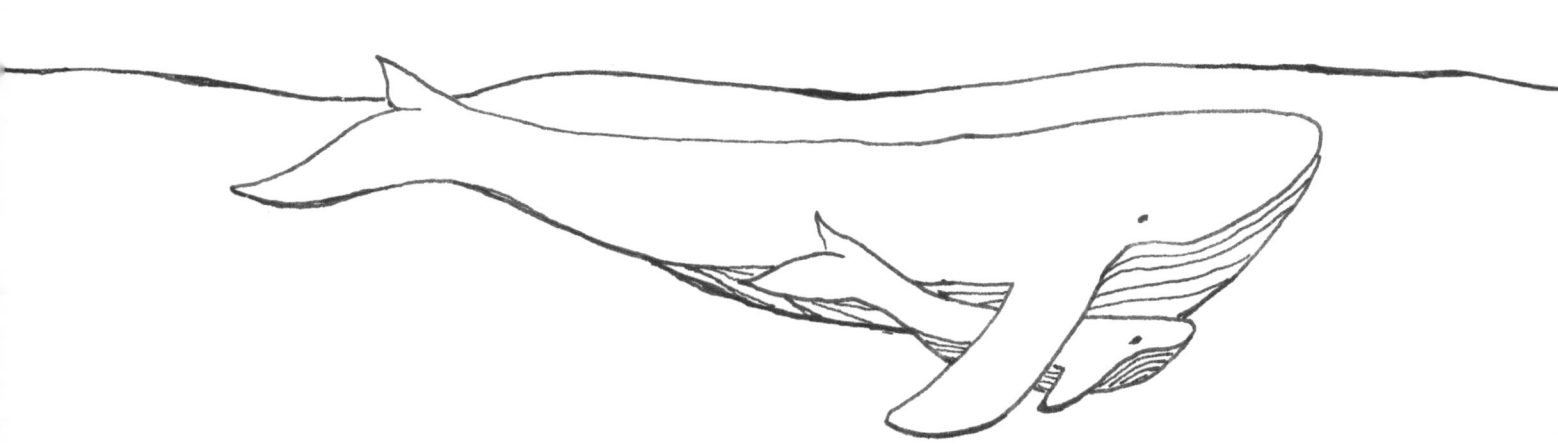

Sun rises; sun sets.
As it did today and every day
that ever was.

Moon rises; moon sets.
As it will tonight and every night
that ever there will be.

Fish Facts

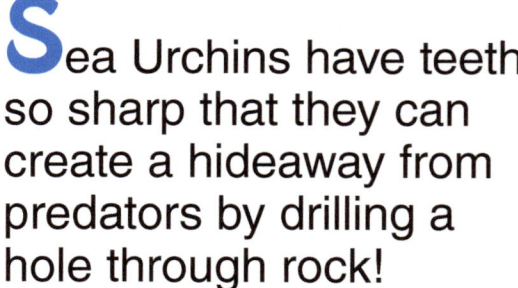

Narwhals are often called the "unicorn of the sea" because the males grow a long tusk from their upper lip.

An adult octopus can squeeze through a hole the size of a dime!

In seahorses, it is the male that carries and delivers babies.

Some jellyfish produce light in their bodies to startle their predators.

Sea Urchins have teeth so sharp that they can create a hideaway from predators by drilling a hole through rock!

Fish travel in schools to trick predators into thinking that they are one large fish.

Swordfish dive deep into the ocean where the water is very cold. They have special organs to raise the temperature of their eyes and brain so they can see their prey better when hunting.

Sting rays have no bones. Their bodies are made of cartilage, which is the squishy stuff found in your nose and ears.

Flying fish can leap out of the water and glide over the ocean using the large fins on the sides of their bodies – just like birds use their wings to soar through the air.

Seals are mammals, so they breathe air just like human beings. Some seals can stay underwater for ½ hour before needing to take a breath!

The blue whale is the largest mammal that has ever lived. Their tongues alone can weigh as much as an elephant!

Horseshoe crabs have 10 eyes! Some eyes are on the horseshoe crab's shell, some are on its tail, and some are near its mouth.

www.ingramcontent.com/pod-product-compliance
Lightning Source LLC
Chambersburg PA
CBHW060814290526
45792CB00005BA/1646